The Way of Everyday Life

Zen Writings Series

The Way of Everyday Life

Zen Master Dogen's Genjokoan with Commentary by Hakuyu Taizan Maezumi

Photographs by John Daido Loori

Foreword by W. S. Merwin
Calligraphy by Vo-Dinh

Zen Writings Series

Series Editors: Hakuyu Taizan Maezumi and Bernard Tetsugen Glassman

On Zen Practice: Foundations of Practice
On Zen Practice II: Body, Breath and Mind
To Forget the Self: An Illustrated Guide to Zen Meditation
The Hazy Moon of Enlightenment: On Zen Practice III
The Way of Everyday Life
Sayings and Doings of Pai-chang (1979)

The Way of Everyday Life, published under the joint auspices of the Zen Center of Los Angeles and the Institute for Transcultural Studies, is one volume in the Zen Writings series, a monographic series comprising two new titles each year. Subscription rate for one year: $10.00 in the U.S. and Canada, $15.00 foreign. For two years: $18.00 in the U.S. and Canada, $28.00 foreign.

For further information, contact: Center Publications, 905 S. Normandie Ave., Los Angeles, California 90006.
© 1978 by Zen Center of Los Angeles, Inc.
Printed in the United States of America.

Library of Congress Cataloguing in Publication Data:

Maezumi, Hakuyu Taizan.
　　　The way of everyday life.

　　　(Zen Writings series; 5)
　　　Includes a translation by H. T. Maezumi and F. Cook of Dogen's essay Genjo koan.
　　　1. Dogen, 1200-1253. Shobo genzo. Genjo koan.
2. Spiritual life (Zen Buddhism)　3. Sotoshu — Doctrines.
I. Dogen, 1200-1253. Shobo genzo. Genjo koan. English.
1978.　II. Title.　III. Series.
BQ9449.D654S53357　　　294.3′4′44　　　78-8309
ISBN 0-916820-06-8

Dedicated to our teachers

CONTENTS

FOREWORD

Here is a direct, spare commentary, by a Zen master of our own time, on a succinct text that we are assured represents the central teaching of one of the greatest figures, and perhaps the most imposing intellect, of Japanese Zen. Those of us who cannot read Dogen in the original, and whose education did not include a familiarity with the cultural background of his writing, must either take the evaluation on faith, or ignore it, at least to begin with. It does not much matter either way, because the sheer authority of Dogen's name will not help us to resolve the crucial questions that are likely to challenge us, upon reading even a few lines of a work such as the *Genjokoan*. Two principal questions, that turn out to one: who is this Dogen (apart from the biographical data and the legends) and what is he saying? The work is over seven centuries old, and in translation, and yet I think that the questions naturally assume the present tense. For these remarkable statements and their source do not seem to be bound to any other moment than the one that presents us with them.

Whatever else Dogen may have meant by the word *koan*, in the title, this work entails some of the difficulty, and promises some of the virtues of koans as they are generally used in Zen practice. Phrase after phrase suggests or assumes two aspects related not by logic but by some deeper implication, and points through both. The problems begin, and perhaps abide, in the words themselves. The English words are not Dogen's, of course, and Dogen's in turn were a translation of the combined intimacy and transcendence that he set out to represent: something which was and is no thing, and which never became the words, yet was never separate from them. Buddhism, and Zen in particular, warns us again and again not to get stuck in the words. The vision, the knowledge, toward which the teachings of Zen claim to direct us are said to be clear beyond any clarity we can hope to describe, but the way to that intuitive certainty does not always appear to be simple. Yet, however involuted the process seems, these words of translation do not exist in order to conduct us into the head of some historical personage, but into an unlimited being that each of us, they tell us, already knows, without being aware of it. Our own essential nature. That Dogen. In words that are nobody's he is speaking not only to us, but, in a sense, from us. Even when what he ways is hard to understand, we can hear that. Each time it is a little different, but each time it is really the same. We recognize it, even if we do not know its name.

Paradox is the agent of most attempts to convey ultimate clarity. I have no notion of what the historical Dogen's humor may have been, but there is a perennial irony in the situation of a work such as this one, which sets out to provide instruction, to make plain, and which fosters from the outset a complex lineage of erudition and explanation. Dogen's writing endures the fate of all poetry that survives. But a commentary such as Maezumi Roshi's is a great and welcome advantage, at present, and for many of us it will seem indispensable. Learned without self-importance or excess baggage. Illuminating, and transparent. Maezumi Roshi is writing from the viewpoint of mature Zen experience to students of Zen, but he does so in a way that makes Dogen more accessible to anyone, acquainted with Zen or not, who wants to listen.

It means listening closely, and not just to the words. Dogen is speaking about the whole thing.

W. S. Merwin

PREFACE

This beautiful book presents in words and images a very simple vision of the great life of which we are a part as essentially good. It makes no extravagant claims or unlikely promises of other worlds, supernatural beings, paranormal powers, and the like. It will not strain your credulity or make impossible demands. Rather, words and photographs collaborate to reveal to us something very basic and truly worthwhile — the nature of our existence and of that greater life we share. Perhaps, after all, that really is extravagant.

There are few people who do not sense some degree of insufficiency within themselves, some barrenness of life and its possibilities. Who has not wished to be more and do more? Yet, it may be that we are good enough to live this life. First, however, we must learn to see clearly. The problem is our perception, for we do not see nearly as well as we think we do. We lack the eye of the artist, and by "artist" I do not mean someone who merely versifies or paints, but someone who can see what the rest of us miss. Real art startles us because it helps us to see that to which we were blind before. Monet's lilies, Warhol's can of soup, Basho's *haiku*, all wake us from our walking stupor and thrust our noses into reality. Complex theories, lofty philosophies, and moralistic and demanding religions to the contrary, all we need to do is to see life with the eye of the artist. If we can do this, then we will find only fullness and richness, not barrenness and deficiency.

This book is not a moral treatise, nor is it at all theoretical or didactic. It does not tell us what we ought to do but instead is itself testimony and proof of the possibility of seeing life with the eye of the artist. Four artists have collaborated, each in his own way, to open our eyes to what we are and to the way to live saner, more integrated lives. The core of the book is an essay entitled *Genjokoan*, loosely translated as "the way of everyday life," composed by the thirteenth-century Zen master Eihei Dogen. This in turn is commented on by a contemporary Zen teacher, Taizan Maezumi Roshi, who is a master in Dogen's lineage. A third collaborator is Daido Loori, whose photographs not only contribute so much to the visual beauty of the book, but are fine representatives of photography as a practice of mindfulness. Finally, the text of *Genjokoan* has been written in calligraphy by the well-known Vietnamese artist Vo-Dinh, whose work also not only adds to the visual power of this book but at the same time is another example of mindfulness in action.

The title of this book, *The Way of Everyday Life*, is very important. First, it points to the fact that it is in this very life — this world — as we live it day by day that we must find ultimate goodness. We need not look beyond this world to other more "spiritual" worlds, future lives, supernatural spirits, or blessed rest in paradise to find that which is absolute reality. We would make a big mistake if we subscribe to an ancient theory that coarse, brute matter masks some spiritual essence. This world, this everyday life, is reality, the total, absolute reality. This is where we must look, and this is where we must learn to live the only life we will have. We all are the Buddha, as are our enemies, the family cat, and the weeds that spring up in the pansy bed.

Second, the title points to the way by which we learn to perceive this world in its fulness and richness. It is a simple practice, and effective, though not easy. It is a process of learning to be at one, unified, with our whole life in its diverse aspects. We need not become involved in ascetic renunciation, radically alter our daily routines, or acquire any arcane knowledge or skill. Instead, as we live our ordinary lives with families, occupations, and daily chores, we learn little by little to affirm each act totally by doing it totally. To do this is to see things clearly, as an artist.

Do not look for complexity in this book, for it is simple, not complex. What Dogen says, and what is repeated in the commentaries and art, is so simple that it is startling, and perhaps it is incredible to those who require omens and portents of miraculous events. The point is this: if we can but see this life without judgment, without evaluation and comparison, we will for the first time begin to see it as it is, and this life will acquire for each of us a quality that greatly surpasses the so-called miraculous and marvellous. What more can we ask? Dogen saw life clearly and in this clear-eyed vision he found the way to live his life. *Genjokoan* is his report to us. When he and the others who have contributed to this book tell us that things are not what they seem but are much more, it seems to me that this is worth listening to. What if they are right?

Maezumi Roshi's commentary is also simple, meant to speak to Californians, New Yorkers, and Alabamans. It contains no esoteric Buddhist terminology, no spiritual obscurities. Because he has learned to see clearly, he is able to clarify Dogen's insight for us, serving as a bridge between different times and places. He does not, that is, speak as a scholar who has read Dogen's writing and then comments from the perspective of the religious historian or historian of ideas, but rather he opens up the *Genjokoan* to us from the perspective of his own deep insight. Consequently, we have two closely related testimonies to the possibilities latent in our everyday life, that of Dogen and that of Maezumi Roshi.

The reader will find it impossible to overlook the photographs which accompany the text, for even to the untrained eye they are striking and beautiful. I wonder if we can really see them? They are not merely illustrations for the text, though they do that; they are themselves a further testimony to the possibility of really learning to see. The scenes are ordinary enough, things we have all seen — stones, trees, people — but they challenge us to look closer, to see them as for the first time, which is, of course, the way an artist sees them. When the lens of the camera opens, the eye of the photographer must be truly open also, and when we look at these pictures, our own eyes must be as open as possible. What do we see then? What do they say to us? If we see little or nothing at all here, we must ask ourselves whether the fault lies with the photographer or ourselves. Is it possible that our own perceptual lens is filtered or capped?

This book, then, attempts to do something other than preach and cajole. Several men assure us in words and images that there is more — More — around us than we imagine. But they also do more than testify: through the words and images we are afforded an opportunity to truly see and hear if we but make the effort.

At the heart of this book is, as I have said, an essay entitled *Genjokoan*, written in the thirteenth century by Zen master Dogen, founder of the Japanese Soto Zen tradition. Does a Japanese Zen master who lived over seven centuries ago have anything to say to a person of our own time and place? I firmly believe he does, because if his words are irrelevant to our lives, then so are the words of Jesus, Socrates, Shakespeare, and many others who came long before us. But it is a mistake to think that we are special by virtue of living long after them, or that our own problems are unique to this time. Human problems, particularly the big ones, never change, and it is very important to remember that Dogen found an ultimate solution.

Of course some of Dogen's problems were unique to his time and culture, as are some of ours, but the essential problem we all face, regardless of time, race, culture, or sex, is the problem of finding a stable basis for our lives in the midst of turmoil, suffering, and struggle. That is the problem stated simply, isn't it? Dogen became aware of this problem very early in his life, partly as a result of losing both parents while he was a child. Out of his own doubts and anxieties developed a long search for this firm basis which we all desire. He found it after many years and a great effort, which led him to become a Buddhist monk, to engage in an intense inner struggle, to make an arduous journey to China, and finally to study with the Chinese Zen master, Ju-ching. Ju-ching helped him to open his own eyes, and when he finally returned to Japan, he returned as Ju-ching's spiritual heir. There, he established Eiheiji Monastery, trained other monks, and composed the ninety-five chapters of *Shobogenzo*, one of the world's great literary, religious, and philosophical documents. *Genjokoan* is the first chapter in that work. In it, he tried to express what he had come to understand.

Basically, his problem is the same problem we all have. He felt that life is unsatisfactory, and like us, he tried to do something about it. So we have this book, in which Dogen and several others from a different age and culture attempt to teach us to see. Can any person afford not to read it carefully, that is, as an artist would? This is a wonderful book, one which is really good for us. I hope you will read it with your eyes open.

Francis Dojun Cook
University of California, Riverside

SHOBOGENZO
GENJO KOAN

by

Zen Master Eihei Dogen

Written in mid-autumn
of the first year of
the Tempuku Era (1233 A.D.)
and given to my lay student
Yo-Koshu of Kyushu.

When all dharmas are buddha-dharma,
there are enlightenment and delusion,
practice, life and death,
buddhas and creatures.

When the ten thousand dharmas
are without self,
there are no delusion, no enlightenment,
no buddhas, no creatures, no life and no death.

The buddha way transcends
being and non-being;
therefore
there are life and death,
delusion and enlightenment,
creatures and buddhas.

Nevertheless,
flowers fall with our attachment,
and weeds spring up
with our aversion.

To carry the self forward
and realize the ten thousand dharmas
is delusion.
That the ten thousand dharmas advance
and realize the self
is enlightenment.

It is buddhas who enlighten delusion.
It is creatures who are deluded in enlightenment.
Further,
there are those who attain enlightenment
above enlightenment;
there are those who are deluded
within delusion.

When buddhas are truly buddhas,
one need not be aware of being buddha.
However,
one is the realized buddha
and further advances
in realizing buddha.

Seeing forms
with the whole body and mind,
hearing sounds
with the whole body and mind,
one understands them
intimately.

Yet it is not
like a mirror with reflections,
nor
like water under the moon --
When
one side
is realized,
the other side
is dark.

To study
the buddha way
is to study the self.
To study the self
is to forget the self.
To forget the self
is to be enlightened by the ten thousand dharmas.
To be enlightened
by the ten thousand dharmas
is to free one's body and mind
and those of others.
No trace
of enlightenment remains,
and this traceless enlightenment
is continued forever.

When one first seeks the truth,
one separates oneself far from its environs.
When one has already correctly
transmitted the truth to oneself,
one is one's original Self at that moment.

When riding on a boat
if one watches the shore
one may assume that the shore is moving.
But watching the boat directly,
one knows that it is the boat that moves.

If one examines the ten thousand dharmas
with a deluded body and mind,
one will suppose that one's mind and nature
are permanent.
But if one practices intimately
and returns to the true Self,
it will be clear
that the ten thousand dharmas
are without Self.

Firewood turns into ash
and does not turn into firewood again.
But do not suppose that the ash is after
and the firewood before.
We must realize that firewood
is in the state of being firewood
and has its before and after.
Yet having this before and after,
it is independent of them.
Ash is in the state of being ash
and has its before and after.
Just as firewood does not become firewood again
after it is ash,
So after one's death
one does not return to life again.

Thus,
that life does not become death
is a confirmed teaching
of the buddha - dharma;
for this reason, life is called the non - born.
That death does not become life
is a confirmed teaching
of the buddha - dharma;
therefore,
death is called the non - extinguished.

Life is a period of itself.
Death is a period of itself.
For example,
they are like winter and spring.
We do not think
that winter becomes spring,
nor do we say
that spring becomes summer.

Gaining enlightenment
is like the moon reflecting in the water.
The moon does not get wet, nor is the water disturbed.
Although its light is extensive and great,
the moon is reflected even in a puddle an inch across.
The whole moon and the whole sky
are reflected in a dew drop in the grass,
in one drop of water.

Enlightenment does not disturb the person,
just as the moon does not disturb the water.
A person does not hinder enlightenment,
just as a dew drop
does not hinder the moon in the sky.
The depth of the drop is the height of the moon.
As for the duration of the reflection
you should examine the water's vastness or smallness,
And you should discern the brightness or dimness
of the heavenly moon.

When the truth does not fill
our body and mind,
we think that we have enough.
When the truth fills our body and mind,
we realize that something is missing.

For example,
when we view the four directions from a boat
on the ocean where no land is in sight,
we see only a circle and nothing else.
No other aspects are apparent.
However, this ocean
is neither round nor square,
and its qualities are infinite in variety.
It is like a palace. It is like a jewel.
It just seems circular
as far as our eyes can reach
at the time.
The ten thousand dharmas
are likewise like this.

Although ordinary life and enlightened life
assume many aspects,
We only recognize and understand
through practice
what the penetrating power
of our vision can reach.
In order to appreciate
the ten thousand dharmas,
We should know
that although they may look round and square,
the other qualities of oceans and mountains
are infinite in variety;
furthermore,
other universes lie in all quarters.
It is so not only around ourselves
but also right here,
and in a single drop of water.

When a fish swims in the ocean,
there is no limit to the water,
no matter how far it swims.
When a bird flies in the sky,
there is no limit to the air,
no matter how far it flies.
However, no fish or bird
has ever left its elements
since the beginning.
When the need is large,
it is used largely.
When the need is small,
it is used in a small way.
Thus, no creature ever
comes short of its own completeness.
Wherever it stands,
it does not fail to cover the ground.

If a bird leaves the air,
it will die at once.
If a fish leaves the water,
it will die at once.
Know, then,
that water is life.
Know
that air is life.
Life is the bird
and life is the fish.
Beyond these
there are further
implications and ramifications.
In this way,
there are
practice and enlightenment,
mortality and immortality.

Now if a bird or a fish tries to reach the limit
of its elements before moving in it,
this bird or this fish will not find
its way or its place.
Attaining this place,
one's daily life is the realization
of ultimate reality (genjo koan).
Attaining this way
one's daily life is the realization
of ultimate reality (genjo koan).
Since this place and this way
are neither large nor small, neither self nor other,
neither existing previously nor just arising now,
they therefore exist thus.

Thus,
if one practices and realizes the buddha way,
when one gains one dharma,
one penetrates one dharma;
when one encounters one action,
one practices one action.

Since the place is here
and the way leads everywhere,
the reason the limits of the Knowable are unKnowable
is simply that our Knowledge arises with,
and practices with,
the absolute perfection of the buddha-dharma.

Do not practice thinking
that realization must become the object
of one's Knowledge and vision
and be grasped conceptually.
Even though the attainment of realization
is immediately manifest,
its intimate nature
is not necessarily realized.
Some may realize it
and some may not.

Priest Pao-ch'e
of Ma-Ku Shan
was fanning himself.
A monk approached and asked,
"Sir, the nature of wind is permanent,
and there is no place it does not reach.
Why, then, must you still fan yourself?"
"Although you understand the nature of wind
is permanent," the master replied,
"you do not understand the meaning
of its reaching everywhere."
"What is the meaning of its reaching everywhere?"
asked the monk.
The master just fanned himself.
The monk bowed with deep respect.

This is the enlightened experience
of buddha-dharma
and the vital way of its correct transmission.
Those who say we should not use a fan
because wind is permanent,
and so we should know the existence of wind
without using a fan,
know neither permanency
nor the nature of wind.
Because the nature of wind
is eternally present,
the wind of Buddhism
actualizes the gold of the earth
and ripens the cheese
of the long river.

The essay Genjokoan *was composed by the Japanese Zen master Eihei Dogen, who lived from 1200 until 1253. Son of aristocratic parents, Dogen developed a strong religious aspiration while still a young boy, partly as a result of the early loss of both parents. Having experienced impermanence and loss while so young, he became a monk at an early age and began a search for the answers to his deepest questionings. The search led him to China, where he was enlightened under the guidance of the Zen master Ju-ching.*

When he returned to Japan, he began a period of great creativity as a teacher and a writer. He established the Japanese Soto Zen tradition, founded the monastery known as Eiheiji, one of the two principal Soto Zen monasteries in Japan, and composed the ninety-five chapters that now make up the Shobogenzo. *This work, of which the present essay is the first chapter, is recognized world-wide as a profound piece of religious literature, and its author is considered by many to have been the most brilliant philosopher Japan has ever produced, as well as a master of prose and poetry and a remarkably well-accomplished spiritual leader.*

Vo-Dinh's calligraphy is in honor of his Father and Mother

INTRODUCTION

Genjokoan, loosely translated, means "the way of everyday life."

Everyday life, of course, is the life we lead from day to day — getting up in the morning, driving to work, going for a run, arguing with a friend. Throughout the day we are relating to many different people, doing various jobs, solving various problems. Actually, this is all there is, just this moment-to-moment life we lead.

But somehow, we're not satisfied, we want something more. Experiencing the death of someone we love, perhaps, or a feeling of alienation from our work or our friends, or just some unidentifiable depression, we begin to wonder about the meaning of life and death. "Who am I really? What am I supposed to be doing? Why am I suffering? What is death?" Deeply questioning, we look outside of ourselves for a way, for a truth to give meaning and wholeness to our lives.

In Zen we talk about the intrinsic and the experiential, two ways of looking at what is essentially one reality. From the intrinsic standpoint, this very ordinary life *is* the way, is perfection itself. If we look for something outside of our immediate situation, outside of ourselves, we are going astray. Intrinsically, the way and everyday life are one and the same. But from the experiential standpoint, we are undeniably dissatisfied. We are unaware of how our life can be true realization, and the way and everyday life seem irreconcilably separate.

Practice is the key to bridging what is in fact an illusory gap. The word *practice* has many rich implications in Zen. In a narrow sense, it refers to the activity of sitting meditation we call **zazen**. To practice zazen means to sit in meditation, concentrating with all our effort until the gap between ourselves and others is eliminated.

In a broader sense, practice refers to the activity of completely involving ourselves in whatever we are doing or experiencing so that there is no gap or separation between ourselves and that activity or experience. It is the extension of zazen into our lives from moment to moment. Usually we separate ourselves from situations: eating a hamburger, we wish we had steak; hearing a sharp word from a friend, we recall all the past times we've been rejected and get terribly depressed; being in pain, we have fantasies of pleasure, and experiencing pleasure, we have fears of pain. When we become aware of this separation, we try to understand it intellectually, seeking a rational explanation or interpretation of our suffering. In fact, by interposing our own concepts and ideas in this way, we are just increasing our distance from things as they are. But when we fully enter into each situation, not looking for something better or remembering something worse, we "forget the self," lose the self in the activity and awaken to the fact that this "self" includes everything. All sense of separation or alienation is eliminated. This awakening is called enlightenment.

The motivation to practice, then, is often this seeming paradox or tension between the intrinsic and the experiential, between the belief that everything is complete and perfect as it is and the fact that we feel a deep dissatisfaction with our lives and want to experience this completeness for ourselves. Of course, ultimately, there is only one reality, and in the *Genjokoan* Master Dogen is constantly shifting perspectives between the intrinsic and the experiential in order to point to that one reality.

Shobogenzo is the name of a larger work of which *Genjokoan* is a part; it literally means "treasury of the true dharma eye," the eye of wisdom which is able to bridge the gap we have been talking about. *Genjokoan* itself can be divided into two principle elements: means "to make real," "to manifest," and so refers to phenomena, to the living of our lives in its most concrete sense. *Koan*, on the other hand, points to the absolute side, to the side of oneness, of completeness. According to one translation, *ko* means "made even or flat," and *an* means "to have its own position." *Genjokoan*, then, means, on one level, that "the position of each thing is absolute." This table, for example, is at once just this table and at the same time the infinite, indestructible universe itself. In the same way, each of us is all reality.

    Genjokoan, then, means that everyday life is realization, everyday life is the way. The term *buddha-dharma* has similar implications. *Buddha* refers to the oneness, to the absolute side, and *dharma* refers to the side of differences. Together they point to the ongoing integration and harmony of oneness and difference which is our life. We can appreciate this life as this physical body, which includes all things, and as the sphere of activity, of living and doing. In either case, the absolute and the relative are inseparable. But it's important to remember that these words, that all words, are only an explanation. We have to verify them with our whole being through practice. Of course, without practice we can survive, but we can never thoroughly understand what Master Dogen is talking about here. When we sit zazen, we are trying to do just that: to see our lives clearly and to identify ourselves with who we really are.

Stephan Ikko Bodian

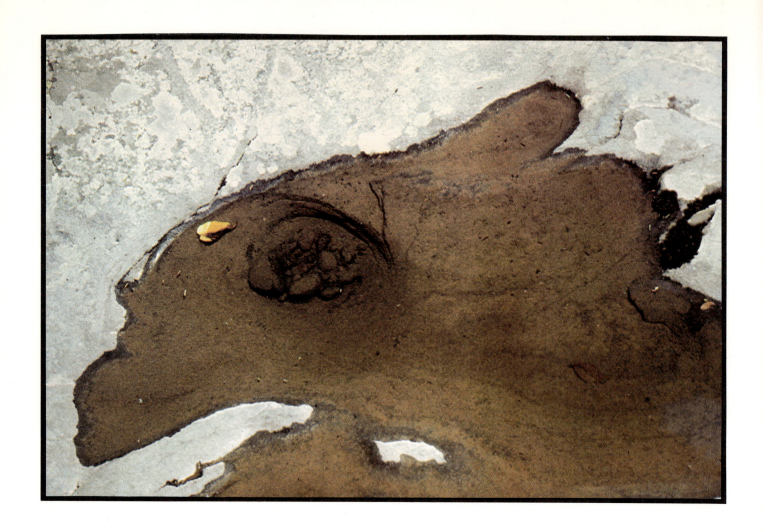

When all dharmas are buddha-dharma, there are
    enlightenment and delusion, practice, life and death,
    buddhas and creatures.
When the ten thousand dharmas are without self,
    there are no delusion, no enlightenment, no
    buddhas, no creatures, no life and no death.
The buddha way transcends being and non-being;
    therefore there are life and death, delusion and
    enlightenment, creatures and buddhas.
Nevertheless,
    flowers fall with our attachment, and weeds
    spring up with our aversion.

COMMENTARY ONE

I thought I'd abandoned all —
Even my body —
And yet this snowy night is cold.

The subject of these first three sentences is our most important concern. To realize this subject, this true self, is the major aim of our practice. As a matter of fact, in Master Dogen's writings the words *we* and *I* are never used; instead, he says simply, "When all dharmas are buddha-dharma." To really understand buddha-dharma is to have a first enlightenment experience, to eliminate this "I" and become aware of who we really are.

That's why we shouldn't overlook this deceptively simple word "when." He doesn't say, "since all dharmas," or simply, "all dharmas," but "when," at the moment we realize that, "all dharmas are buddha-dharma." It's like a person with a pocketful of money starving to death in front of a restaurant because he's unaware of the money in his pocket. Intrinsically, all dharmas are buddha-dharma, but until we realize it, for us it's not true.

The usual way of understanding the first three sentences is to see them as a progression from affirmation to negation to integration or transcendence. According to this interpretation, the first sentence describes our discriminating awareness before enlightenment, the second the first experience of oneness, and the third the realm of subtle differences we are able to perceive after enlightenment.

However, if we only appreciate it in that way we lose Master Dogen's intent. Actually each sentence is also saying the same thing from different perspectives. For example, we can say, "When all dharmas are buddha-dharma, there are *no* enlightenment, *no* delusion, *no* buddhas, *no* creatures, *no* life and *no* death," because everything is buddha-dharma, everything is reality itself, everything is genjokoan. Since everything is this one reality, there are no delusion, no enlightenment, no life and no death apart from it. To see this, to identify ourselves with all phenomena, is enlightenment.

When we become really selfless in this way, all suffering, happiness, mountains, stars, trees, grasses and people become nothing but the self. What does that really mean? We call it "emptiness," not empty in the sense of void or insubstantial, but in the sense of empty of any fixed character or self, constantly changing, unconditioned. This is not some special state, but the fundamental nature of our lives.

We usually appreciate things in a dualistic way by separating ourselves from them. Then a gap appears, and into that gap fall greed, anger, ignorance and the various other ideas and emotions that disturb us. But when we really make ourselves empty and realize that everything is nothing but the self, the gap is eliminated and we see phenomena as they are.

Another way to clarify the first three sentences is to use the analogy of waves and water. Seeing reality according to the perspective of the first sentence is like looking at the ocean and seeing the waves. We are aware the ocean is there, but our attention is on the waves, the various phenomena that make up our lives. In the next sentence the emphasis is on the water, the ground of being, emptiness, the absolute. And in the last sentence we go beyond the duality of waves and water entirely and see them both together as one indivisible reality. All along, of course, we are looking at the same ocean; only our perspective is changing.

"Before this old monk studied Zen twenty years ago, seeing a mountain, the mountain was a mountain; seeing water, the water was water. Later, I met my teacher and attained some realization. Then a mountain was no longer a mountain, water no longer water. Now after further accomplishment, seeing a mountain, mountain is mountain; seeing water, water is water. I ask you, are these three views the same or different? If you can answer, you'll meet me intimately."
— Ch'in-yuan Wei-hsin (Seigen Ishin)

Nevertheless, flowers fall with our attachment, and weeds spring up with our aversion.

Nevertheless,
*   flowers fall with our attachment,*
*   and weeds spring up with our aversion.*

To carry the self forward and realize the ten thousand dharmas is delusion.

That the ten thousand dharmas advance and realize the self is enlightenment.

It is buddhas who enlighten delusion.

It is creatures who are deluded in enlightenment.

Further, there are those who attain enlightenment above enlightenment; there are those who are deluded within delusion.

When buddhas are truly buddhas, one need not be aware of being buddha.

However, one is the realized buddha and further advances in realizing buddha.

COMMENTARY TWO

A full bottle makes no sound.

"To carry the self" means to look for something outside of yourself. Right there a dichotomy arises. No matter how much you practice, still a gap remains, and even enlightenment can become a hindrance by which you increase the separation between yourself and others. That is one of the sicknesses of Zen.

"That the ten thousand dharmas advance," on the other hand, means that, merging yourself into the object, the objective world itself becomes your life. In this very body and its functioning, abundant life and total liberation are constantly manifesting. To actualize and advance in this way is our practice.

To try to seek after enlightenment, then, is delusion, and yet enlightenment is crucial. In fact, the most common mistake we make is that without knowing what enlightenment is, we oversimplify, we overgeneralize, confusing ourselves and others. To say that we're all enlightened is easy, but to realize it clearly is not easy at all.

Even within Zen, we have many levels of realization, of enlightenment. For example, there are the ten oxherding pictures, in which the ox represents true nature. True enlightenment begins with the fourth stage, "catching the ox," grasping true nature, yet most of us are still stuck in the stage of "seeing the traces." Even among those who have been practicing for many years, most are still barely at the third stage of "seeing the ox." So our practice is endless, and there are innumerable levels we can achieve.

Of course all of us without exception are wonderful bodhisattvas ("enlightenment-beings"); whether we have had an enlightenment experience or not is not so significant. We are all bodhisattvas who strive for higher, clearer realization. That is our practice. It's quite all right to be deluded. I'm more than willing to be deluded. That is our way.

One Zen master said, "It is buddhas who enlighten delusion where there is no delusion at all. It is people who are deluded in enlightenment where there is no enlightenment at all." Delusion where there is no delusion at all. Enlightenment where there is no enlightenment at all. What's the difference? Aren't they the same? But if we take enlightenment and delusion as separate, buddhas and ourselves become separate as well. We are not at all separate to begin with, so why do we have difficulty? Flowers fall. Is it because of our attachment? Weeds spring up. Is it because we hate them?

If you really identify yourself with everything else, you identify yourself with enlightenment also. In other words, enlightenment is nothing but you yourself. You just do whatever you do, and there is nothing extra, no problem involved to upset or disturb you. In that case, as Zen Master Lin-chi (Rinzai) used to say, "Living in hell is like taking a walk in a beautiful park."

When you really become delusion itself, when only delusion exists, then there is no longer any delusion, for there is nothing apart from delusion. But as long as this remains just your idea, it's not true delusion within delusion. That's why it's crucial to experience such a state for yourself. We have a saying, "Fire can't burn fire." You have to become fire yourself.

"Attain enlightenment above enlightenment." We progress in that way, stage by stage, building up clarity upon clarity, wisdom upon wisdom, making the illumination of wisdom brighter and stronger.

"Deluded within delusion." The more we realize, the more compassionate we become, and the more compassionate we become, the more deluded we have to be.

When all beings are wallowing in the mud, we have to jump into the mud to be with them. Just sitting back, we can't accomplish much. And obviously, when we get into the mud, we become muddy. That's being deluded within delusion. That's our life.

When we are buddha, we don't necessarily recognize that we are buddha. In fact, as the historical Buddha Shakyamuni himself realized, everything without exception is the buddha. Or as Zen Master Hakuin said, "Apart from sentient beings there are no buddhas. Apart from buddhas there are no sentient beings."

One of my teachers used to say, "Make your mind empty. Right there is the buddha." When we are involved in doing something, we should put ourselves completely into it. Reading, working, even laughing or crying. When we cry, we're crying buddha; when we laugh, we're laughing buddha.

But until we realize this, we're not convinced. Of course we don't have to say, "Now I'm the buddha." If you consciously recognize it in that way, there is something you have become which is different from who you were, and already you've started creating duality where there is none. We often use the expression, "Fire doesn't burn fire. The eye doesn't see the eye." Similarly, when the stomach is healthy, you are not aware of its functioning: "When buddhas are truly buddhas, one need not be aware of being buddha."

The etymological root of *buddha* is *budh*, "to awaken." When we really awaken we become the buddha, regardless of race or sex or age. The point of our practice is to accomplish this awakening.

"Further advance in realizing buddha." Our practice and our accomplishment are as endless and as boundless as the universe. Shakyamuni Buddha himself says, "The three worlds are nothing but my possession, and all beings are nothing but my children." Isn't it wonderful? What he means is that we should take care of everybody and everything else in the same way that we take care of ourselves. In other words, to see everything else as part of ourselves is wisdom. And when wisdom is truly realized, then compassion, loving-kindness, spontaneously arises as the functioning of that wisdom.

In Zen we speak of three different kinds of compassion. The first is "compassion toward beings," compassion as it is most commonly understood: seeing other people suffering, you want to do as much as you can to help them, both by removing their suffering and by giving them comfort. The second, "compassion toward dharmas (phenomena)," reflects a more advanced stage of understanding and practice: having wisdom, you see that beings and objects are not really existing in the usual sense, as something substantial and apart from you. That being the case, to hope to do something to save them is also a delusion, and yet having that delusion, you still do the deluded work of saving others. The last one is the ideal way of being compassionate: having no particular relation to others, what you do very naturally, spontaneously becomes beneficial to them. When you are really selfless, it just happens aimlessly in that way.

To carry the self forward and realize the ten thousand dharmas
is delusion.
That the ten thousand dharmas advance and realize the self is
enlightenment.

*Seeing forms with the whole body and mind, hearing
    sounds with the whole body and mind, one
        understands them intimately.
Yet it is not like a mirror with reflections, nor like water
        under the moon —
When one side is realized, the other side is dark.*

COMMENTARY THREE

"Seeing forms with the whole body and mind, hearing sounds with the whole body and mind."

This refers to the moment of enlightenment. For one Zen master it occurred at the sight of peach blossoms, for another at the sound of a pebble striking bamboo. Please don't get the idea, though, that "seeing forms with the whole body and mind" is something only Zen masters experience, something exotic and impossible to attain. On the contrary, many of you will have the same experience. For example, one of my teacher's students, an American woman, was enlightened before she had even heard of Zen while gazing intently at a desk in front of her. Up until that point she had been concentrating on the question, "What is life?" and her awakening occurred as a natural outgrowth of her practice.

Relating this to yourself, you can see how you should pursue your life. Whatever practice you are involved in, whatever work you are doing—even reading my words right now or looking at the photographs on the pages that follow—absorb yourself totally into it with whole body and mind. Just continue in this way, and when the time comes, you will see that it is all true, that your very life is the life of the enlightened one.

Later on in the *Genjokoan* Master Dogen uses the metaphor of the moon reflected in the water to explain enlightenment. In that instance, the moon is true self reflected on the surface of mind. If the mind is disturbed, true nature will not be apparent, just as agitated water will not reflect the light of the moon. But here Master Dogen says it is "*not* like…water under the moon" because there is no such object, no such true self, no such moon outside of ourselves to be reflected. Nothing exists but that moon, and that is who we are. When we call it "moon," we disappear. When we call it "I," the moon disappears. When there is just this true self, this one reality, nothing else exists besides that.

"When one side is realized, the other side is dark" means that this one side contains everything, without confusion or duality. Usually "dark" has the sense of "ignorant," but here it rather has the sense of "all-inclusive." When we've realized "one side," we are able to function quite freely in the realm of that "other side" which Master Dogen calls "dark." Actually, whether we call it "light" or "dark" is not so important. Being one with whatever we are doing, wherever we are right now—washing the dishes, listening to the sounds of birds— that is our whole life right there. Being one, we become infinite. We become zero. That is what is meant by "to forget the self" and "to be enlightened by all things."

Seeing forms with the whole body and mind,
  hearing sounds with the whole body and mind, one understands
  them intimately.

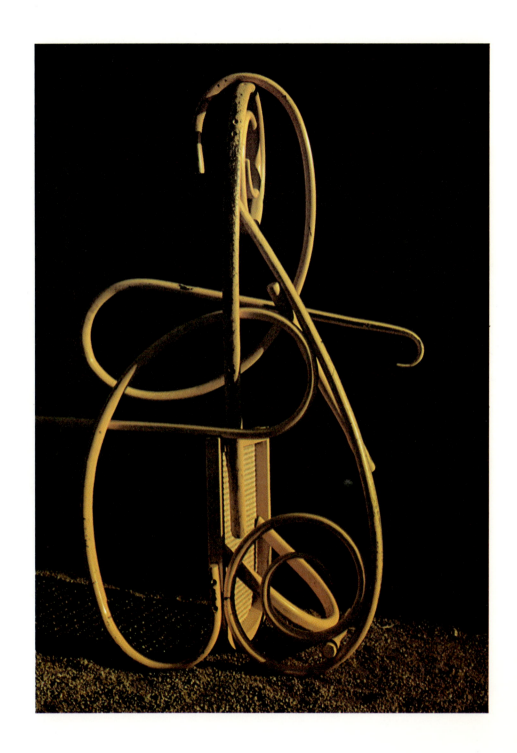

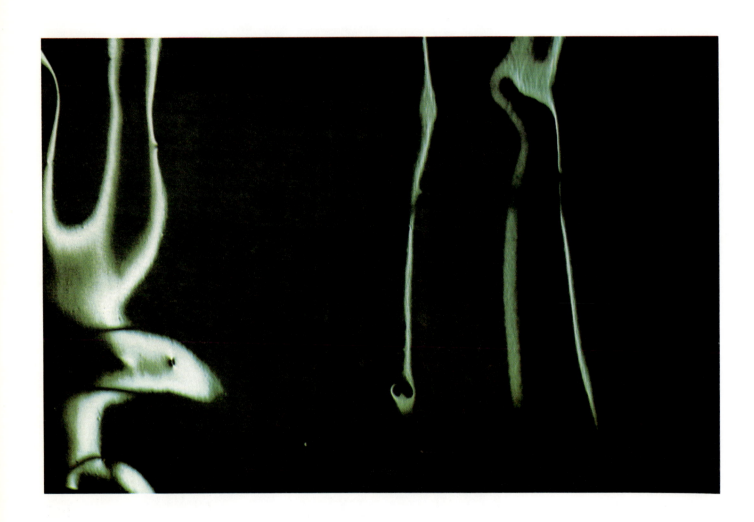

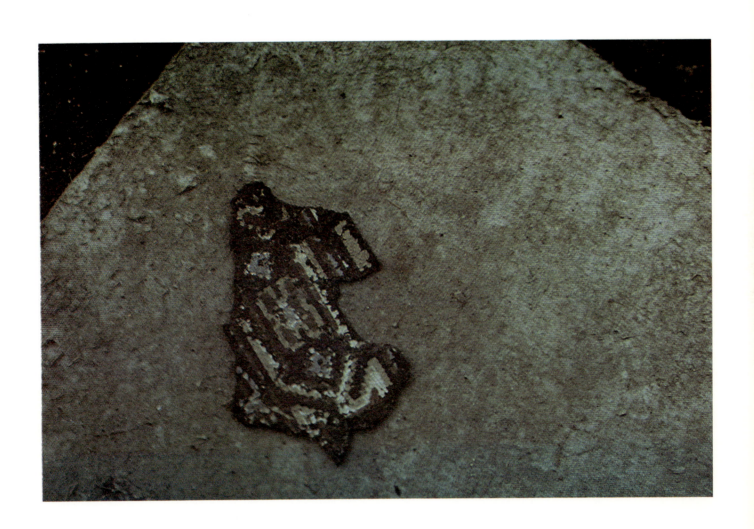

To study the buddha way is to study the self.
To study the self is to forget the self.
To forget the self is to be enlightened by the ten
    thousand dharmas.
To be enlightened by the ten thousand dharmas is to
    free one's body and mind and those of others.
No trace of enlightenment remains, and this traceless
    enlightenment is continued forever.

COMMENTARY FOUR

The buddha way is right beneath your feet.

"To study the buddha way is to study the self." Remove "to study." Then what is left? "The buddha way is the self." What is the self? The buddha way. Who are you? Who is buddha? How can we realize buddha? By forgetting the self.

Now let's eliminate "the buddha way" and "the self." "To study is to study." Discipline is discipline. Enlightenment is enlightenment. Delusion is delusion. Life is life. But always we experience a separation, and that causes problems.

Someone recently asked me, "What is discipline?" To study the buddha way is discipline. To know the self is discipline. To realize that the buddha way is the self is discipline. Become awakened — that's discipline. Really know who you are — that's discipline. That is what is meant by "to forget the self." Really be yourself. When you are so, you will be enlightened by all things. Everything in your life from morning to night becomes the enlightened life. Isn't it simple?

Unfortunately, the self we usually talk about is not the real self, but rather an illusion, a concept, a shadow. To perceive something through the senses is not real perception. But we perceive it in that way, a part of our consciousness starts doing

something with it — interpreting, evaluating, analyzing, criticizing — and then we formulate our own opinions or ideas about it. All of these intellectual functions are based on our knowledge and on our experiences, which are partial and limited. Consequently, whatever we draw from them is also limited. For example, the more learned a scholar is, the more refined, complicated and sophisticated his work may be, but fundamentally it's still illusion.

To forget the self is to go beyond these limitations by eliminating the subject-object relationship and perceiving reality directly. That is what is meant by being "without self." That's our practice. Just sit right and totally absorb yourself in sitting, become sitting itself, and the subject-object dichotomy will fall away.

In Zen we often practice by using koans, penetrating questions or situational problems which we can't understand intellectually. "Who am I?" for example, is an excellent koan. In fact, we practice together precisely in order to find out the answer to that koan.

Working on a koan like "Who am I?" you have to allow "Who am I?" to occupy you completely. As long as you and "Who am I?" are separate, it's still a relative or dualistic state. Putting yourself completely into it, you will even forget about being one with "Who am I?" — you yourself will be forgotten. Then nothing but "Who am I?" exists, and this "Who am I?" is absolute. At this point your true nature will show its face, and you will have a glimpse of who you really are. That's what "To forget the self is to be enlightened by all things" means.

"To be enlightened by the ten thousand dharmas is to free one's body and mind and those of others."

Free has interesting implications. First there is the sense of free in *freedom* : unrestricted, unhindered, liberated. Then we also have the implication in English of "without conditions, without taking anything back," as in, "I give this to you free." Just to give, that's the true spirit of *free*. When you sit in meditation, just sit freely and fully without any expectations or restrictions. Sitting freely, you can make yourself free.

"No trace of enlightenment…" Intrinsically, all of us at this very moment are the buddha. We are in the midst of enlightenment and are leaving no trace. "Leaving no trace" means that in each moment we are newly being born and newly dying. But experientially the question is, How are we perceiving and reacting to situations? Are we holding on to what we see and hear? Do we carry yesterday's emotion into today's relationship? Intrinsically, it's so obvious that "this traceless enlightenment continues forever," but experientially it's up to us to practice and realize it for ourselves.

"There is an easy way to become buddha: do not commit evil, rid the mind of attachment to life and death, be compassionate to all sentient beings, respect your elders and take good care of your juniors, rid the mind of all cravings and aversions, think of nothing and worry about nothing. This is called buddha. Don't seek anything other than this."

— Zen Master Dogen
Shobogenzo: Shoji

No trace of enlightenment remains, and this traceless enlightenment is continued forever.

*When one first seeks the truth, one separates oneself
    far from its environs.*

*When one has already correctly transmitted the truth
    to oneself, one is one's original self at that
    moment.*

*When riding on a boat, if one watches the shore one
    may assume that the shore is moving.*

*But watching the boat directly, one knows that it is the
    boat that moves.*

*If one examines the ten thousand dharmas with a
    deluded body and mind, one will suppose that
    one's mind and nature are permanent.*

*But if one practices intimately and returns to the true
    self, it will be clear that the ten thousand dharmas
    are without self.*

COMMENTARY FIVE

In Buddhism we have three fundamental principles which we call the three dharma marks: everything is impermanent; everything is no-self; and everything is nirvana (tranquility or peace). In fact, in China when they translated a scripture, they would use these three marks as the criteria to determine whether or not the scripture was the authentic teaching of the Buddha.

The first mark means that everything is constantly changing, nothing is fixed. For example, it has become clear to modern physics that reality is composed of innumerable tiny particles, some of which last only a very small fraction of a second. According to the Heisenberg uncertainty principle, it has been shown that when we try to measure the behavior of such particles, we alter the way in which they interact. On the physiological levels, cells are constantly dying and being replaced, and within seven years the entire body has been completely renewed. In relationships among people, when we are close to a person who is joyful, we feel joyful too; when we are close to someone who is sad, we become sad ourselves. From moment to moment, from day to day, our moods change without any apparent cause. Intrinsically, impermanence is the nature of things. At a psychological level, impermanence takes the form of uncertainty, insecurity and a desire to find something dependable and absolute. That is why we practice, to discover the truth upon which we can rely.

Master Dogen himself lost his father when he was three years old and his mother when he was seven. It is said that at the sight of the smoke rising from the incense burning beside his mother's coffin, he became deeply aware of the impermanence of life. This was his primary motivation for becoming a monk.

The second mark, "everything is no-self," is a natural outgrowth of the first. Since nothing is fixed, the so-called self doesn't really exist. What we think of as our self is actually a constellation of feelings, thoughts, sensations, and so on, that are constantly changing from moment to moment. Since there is no self, there is nothing to gain and nothing to lose—for who is there to gain or lose? That being the case, there is nothing to worry about either. Fully realizing this no-self is the third dharma mark, nirvana, the extinction of all our troublesome desires, which is itself tranquility and peace. That's what Master Dogen is saying here. "Practice intimately and return to the true self…" That true self is no-self, and no self is nirvana. Having this body and mind, these thoughts, sensations and feelings, we are actively involved in life but are neither attached to nor detached from it. If we can live like that, we are already in nirvana.

"When one first seeks the truth, one separates oneself far from its environs. When one has already correctly transmitted the truth to oneself, one is one's original self at that moment."

When you seek after enlightenment, enlightenment will elude you. Yet without seeking after it, you will never realize it. Buddha uses the analogy of the millionaire's son who, having forgotten who he is, starts wandering as a beggar from place to place. After many years spent wandering in this way, trying to discover his identity, he finally arrives at his original home and suddenly remembers who he is. We are like that. When we really discover our true self, our treasurehouse will open and we will use it at will.

To realize that there is nothing to transmit is "correct transmission." In other words, full appreciation, full realization of being yourself. If you put an extra head on top of your own, you will become a monstrosity.

When we talk about self and original self, it sounds as if they were two different things, but actually they're one and the same. The content of that oneness is emptiness, not a blank, hollow state, but total fullness. On the other hand, when we experience ourselves as separate from externals, we are far away from the truth. That's what delusion means.

But if one practices intimately and returns to the true self, it will be clear that the ten thousand dharmas are without self.

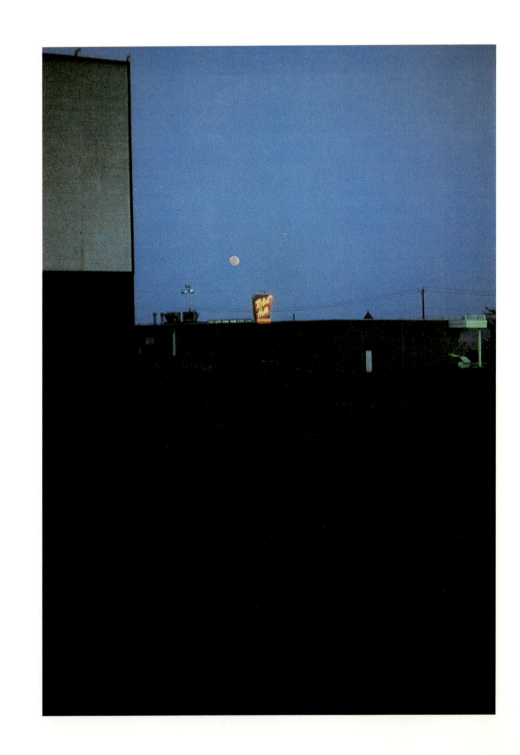

*Firewood turns into ash and does not turn into
    firewood again.*
*But do not suppose that the ash is after and the
    firewood is before.*
*We must realize that firewood is in the state of being
    firewood and has its before and after. Yet having
    this before and after, it is independent of them.*
*Ash is in the state of being ash and has its before and
    after.*
*Just as firewood does not become firewood again after
    it is ash, so after one's death one does not return to
    life again.*
*Thus, that life does not become death is a confirmed
    teaching of the buddha-dharma; for this reason,
    life is called the non-born.*
*That death does not become life is a confirmed
    teaching of the buddha-dharma; therefore, death
    is called the non-extinguished.*
Life is a period of itself.
Death is a period of itself.
For example, they are like winter and spring.
*We do not think that winter becomes spring, nor do we
    say that spring becomes summer.*

COMMENTARY SIX

When you live, just live.
When you die, just die.

Commonly, two views are held concerning life and death. According to the first, although our physical body is destroyed, we have a soul or spirit which goes someplace else and continues to exist. From Master Dogen's time until today, this has been a popular point of view. The other commonly-held view is that when a person dies he or she simply ceases to exist.

In Buddhism, body and mind are not considered two but one, so there is no separate spirit which continues after death. Of course we don't deny the existence of a life after death, and there are Buddhist theories involving reincarnation, karma and the various realms into which one might be reborn. But all of these can be explained in terms of the present moment.

As far as our common sense goes, we think that we have had a past, are having a present and are going to have a future, that there is something which persists through all of these. But actually, each moment, each instant, is totally absolute, and past and future are included in it. That total, absolute life of each moment dies and is reborn unceasingly.

Traditionally it is said that each twenty-four hours contains 649,998,000 separate instants. If we look at them closely, we see that life and death as we usually think of them do not exist at all. That's why they're called "non-born" and "non-extinguished."

For example, if you take a lighted stick of incense and rotate it in the darkness, you will see a very clear circle. Is it alive? Is it an unbroken circle? In a way, yes, and in a way, no. We think we see continuity, but it is all an illusion. It's like a movie. We see continuous motion, but actually each frame is totally independent. Our life is like that.

Therefore, not only does life not become death, but this very moment of life does not become the life of the next moment. There is nothing persistent which can come to an end, nothing to gain and nothing to lose. Isn't it wonderful?

A life which has never been born and will never be extinguished, a life which is absolutely life, that's what our life is. The extent to which one has studied or accomplished is rather secondary. All of us are equally absolute, equally precious, equally splendid, wherever we are at this moment.

Life is a period of itself.
Death is a period of itself.
For example, they are like winter and spring.
    We do not think that winter becomes spring, nor do we
    say that spring becomes summer.

Gaining enlightenment is like the moon reflecting in
the water.
The moon does not get wet, nor is the water disturbed.
Although its light is extensive and great, the moon is
reflected even in a puddle an inch across.
The whole moon and the whole sky are reflected in a
dew-drop in the grass, in one drop of water.
Enlightenment does not disturb the person, just as the
moon does not disturb the water.

A person does not hinder enlightenment, just as a dew-
drop does not hinder the moon in the sky.
The depth of the drop is the height of the moon.
As for the duration of the reflection, you should
examine the water's vastness or smallness,
And you should discern the brightness or dimness of
the heavenly moon.

COMMENTARY SEVEN

The moon goes down
My shadow becomes me.

In an earlier passage Master Dogen said that the moment of enlightenment is "not like a mirror with reflections nor like water under the moon." Here he says, "Gaining enlightenment is like the moon reflecting in the water"; nevertheless, he is not contradicting himself. An analogy is always partial; no analogy covers every aspect. In the first passage he is talking about the very state of enlightenment: when you say "moon," the whole world is that moon; when you say "water," that water occupies the whole world. Nothing else but moon, nothing else but water. If we recognize something outside of ourselves, we become separate from our true nature just as the moon is separate from the water. That is why he says, "when one side is realized, the other side is dark." When we become completely one with the moon or the water, there is nothing outside of that moon or that water.

In the Soto school of Zen we tend to emphasize the intrinsic aspect of practice and enlightenment: we are all already enlightenment itself, so there is no need to seek it outside of ourselves. Definitely this is true, but first we have to pass through the stage of seeking it. In our daily life, we are using wisdom from morning to night: we get up, eat, go to work, and when the time comes we come back, eat dinner, enjoy ourselves, go to bed—nothing but the functioning of wisdom. And yet in the midst of that wisdom we are deluded by our ideas and views which arise from our ego-consciousness and separate us from others. In this way we create problems for ourselves.

If we were totally and absolutely contented and satisfied with ourselves as we are, there would be nothing more to say. But somehow our discursive, dualistic way of looking at things is so deeply rooted, our ego-consciousness is so stubborn, that we've got to do something about it experientially. The moon is not actually separate from us, but somehow it seems to be. Until we see it reflected in the still water of our minds, we can't be satisfied.

"Although its light is extensive and great, the moon is reflected even in a puddle an inch across. The whole moon and the whole sky are reflected in a dewdrop in the grass, in one drop of water."

Here Master Dogen is talking about the various degrees of realization. Enlightenment itself is boundless, but each of us realizes it to a greater or lesser extent. Yet great or small, enlightenment is enlightenment, the moon's reflection is the moon's reflection. "Enlightenment does not disturb the person…" because they can't be separated, they are not two separate things.

"The depth of the drop" is one's achievement in practice, one's understanding and clarity, which is equivalent to the light of the moon. The deeper one's realization, the brighter the moon will shine. On the other hand, we hinder ourselves because of our limited, shallow understanding. Depending on whether or not it's ego-centered, that same understanding can become the wisdom to guide our lives or can become a hindrance, causing us difficulty and pain.

In Buddhism, the term for ignorance literally means "no light." Having no light, we don't know where to go, and not knowing where to go, we bump into things, causing trouble for ourselves and others. Experientially, we can deepen our lives, deepen our understanding through practice; intrinsically, our lives already have a certain depth, a certain light, and by our practice we allow that light to shine forth.

Although its light is extensive and great, the moon is reflected
even in a puddle an inch across.
The whole moon and the whole sky are reflected in a dew-drop
in the grass, in one drop of water.

When the truth does not fill our body and mind, we
think that we have enough.
When the truth fills our body and mind, we realize that
something is missing.
For example, when we view the four directions from a
boat on the ocean where no land is in sight, we see
only a circle and nothing else.
No other aspects are apparent.
However, this ocean is neither round nor square, and
its qualities are infinite in variety. It is like a
palace. It is like a jewel. It just seems circular as
far as our eyes can reach at the time.
The ten thousand dharmas are likewise like this.
Although ordinary life and enlightened life assume
many aspects, we only recognize and understand
through practice what the penetrating power of
our vision can reach.
In order to appreciate the ten thousand dharmas, we
should know that although they may look round
or square, the other qualities of oceans and
mountains are infinite in variety; furthermore,
other universes lie in all quarters.
It is so not only around ourselves but also right here,
and in a single drop of water.

COMMENTARY EIGHT

"When the truth does not fill our body and mind, we think that we have enough. When the truth fills our body and mind, we realize that something is missing."

You might consider such statements strange because they seem to involve a contradiction. Ordinarily we think, "When the truth does *not* fill our body and mind, we think that it is not enough." In fact, some of you may believe that the reason you practice zazen is to fill your body and mind with the truth until you feel your understanding is adequate.

What actually happens is that after the first enlightenment experience, in which you feel as if you occupy the whole universe, you become somewhat arrogant and overestimate your accomplishment. Of course, that's a necessary stage to pass through, but as long as you think you've accomplished enough, it's not true accomplishment. The deeper your realization and the clearer your wisdom, the more clearly you see how much there is for you to do. In this way, wisdom gives rise to compassion.

"We see only a circle and nothing else."

Circles stand for perfection, completeness, and in that sense, each one of us is a circle, particularly when we do zazen. If you really spin a top well, you can't tell whether or not the top is moving. In fact, in Japan the children say that a perfectly spinning top becomes transparent and disappears. Our zazen is like that. If we really sit well, the self disappears and we become a boundless circle that includes everything. How small it is, how big it is, how clear it is, depends on the power of our vision.

The ocean's features, for example, are truly infinite in variety: all kinds of creatures live on the bottom, fish and sea-mammals swim at all depths, coral and rocks and seaweed abound. Traditionally we say that to a fish the ocean appears to be a great palace, and to a heavenly creature it looks like a jewel. Yet riding on the surface, all we can see is the vast expanse of ocean. By our practice, we penetrate the surface of this ocean and begin to see its innumerable qualities for ourselves.

"Although ordinary life and enlightened life may assume many aspects."

What we have translated as "ordinary life" literally means "six dusts," the objective world which we perceive through our senses and consciousness. We call them dusts because they defile our fundamental subjective condition, which is intrinsically pure. For example, when we see something pretty, we attach to it, and that attachment becomes a defilement. Of course, there is nothing intrinscially defiling about the senses themselves, but we are conditioned to react in a certain way to what we perceive. That is the ordinary way of living, which is rather deluded, rather unenlightened.

On the other hand, the enlightened state is the state in which we forget the self and are enlightened by all things, identify ourselves with all things. In this state, there is no way in which our perceptions can be a defilement, because things are not perceived as separate from ourselves.

Although they may look round or square, the other
qualities of oceans and mountains are infinite in variety;
furthermore, other universes lie in all quarters.

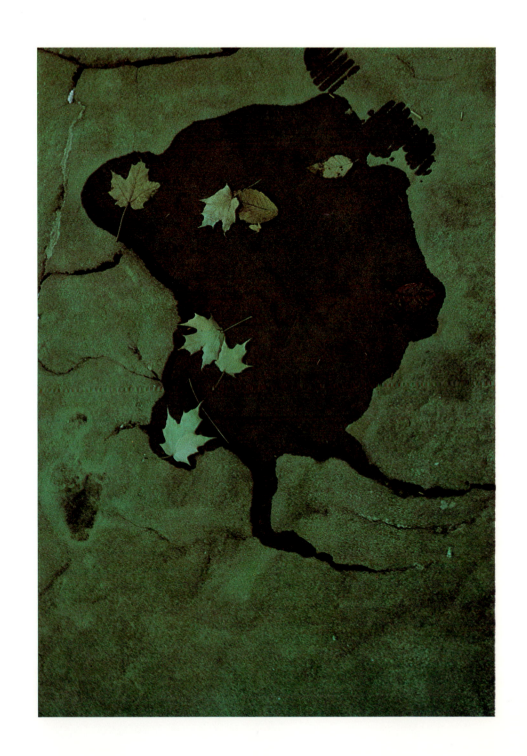

When a fish swims in the ocean, there is no limit to
    the water, no matter how far it swims.
When a bird flies in the sky, there is no limit to the air,
    no matter how far it flies.
However, no fish or bird has ever left its element since
    the beginning.
When the need is large, it is used largely.
When the need is small, it is used in a small way.
Thus, no creature ever comes short of its own
    completeness.
Wherever it stands, it does not fail to cover the ground.
If a bird leaves the air, it will die at once.
If a fish leaves the water, it will die at once.
Know, then, that water is life.
Know that air is life.
Life is the bird and life is the fish.
Beyond these, there are further implications and
    ramifications.
In this way, there are practice and enlightenment,
    mortality and immortality.

COMMENTARY NINE

The thought-cluttered bucket's bottom is broken;
Neither water nor moon remain.

True nature is the air for us, it is the air, water, fire and wind for us. Just as a fish can't survive without water and a bird can't survive without air, without true nature we can't survive. In fact, true nature is our life. Those of you who are struggling to understand this true nature are like birds who are in the air but do not recognize that fact. The bird is air, air is the bird. True nature is you, you are true nature. Everything is true nature. Usually we think that the bird and the air are separate. It's amazing to see how deeply deluded we are.

Put the word *emptiness* in place of *life*. Know that water is emptiness, know that air is emptiness, that we are emptiness, emptiness is everything. This emptiness is the same as "without self." When all dharmas are without self, we see that water is life and air is life, life is the bird and life is the fish. But leaving emptiness we'll die at once. Can't we see? Our practice is to realize this fact.

In another sense, emptiness is boundlessness, what Master Dogen refers to when he says, "there is no limit to the air . . . no limit to the water." Since our life itself is empty, it has no limit. If it's large, we use it largely; if it's small, we use it in a small way. When we recognize some limitation, we are limiting ourselves.

"When the need is large it is used largely. When the need is small it is used in a small way."

Large and small: what scale can we use to compare them? Each is absolute and complete in itself. A big bird is not necessarily superior to a small bird. Each has its own function, its own place. That's why Master Dogen says, "No creature ever comes short of its own completeness. Wherever it stands it does not fail to cover the ground." Life is completely contained in you. Being as we are, right here, right now, can we call it large or small? The terms *large* and *small* just don't reach to it.

"However, no fish or bird has ever left its element since the beginning."

In the same way, human beings never leave enlightenment, and no matter how much we use, there is always enough. In fact, just as "the depth of the drop is the height of the moon," the more we practice, the more deeply we realize the nature of our lives. And just as the moon and the water don't hinder one another, life and realization are perfectly interfused.

Thus, no creature ever comes short of its own completeness.
Wherever it stands, it does not fail to cover the ground.

*Now if a bird or a fish tries to reach the limit of its
    element before moving in it, this bird or this fish
    will not find its way or its place.*

*Attaining this place, one's daily life is the realization of
    ultimate reality (genjokoan). Attaining this way,
    one's daily life is the realization of ultimate reality
    (genjokoan).*

*Since this place and this way are neither large nor
    small, neither self nor other, neither existing
    previously nor just arising now, they therefore
    exist thus.*

*Thus, if one practices and realizes the buddha way,
    when one gains one dharma, one penetrates one
    dharma; when one encounters one action, one
    practices one action.*

COMMENTARY TEN

"Now if a bird or a fish tries to reach the limit of its element before moving in it, this bird or this fish will not find its way or its place."

We are living the abundant life which we call buddha-nature or true self. If we try to measure it before we start practicing, it is almost as if, putting living aside, we were to try to find out the meaning of life. Actually, the only way we can discover its meaning is by living and appreciating this life.

In the case of the bird and the fish, it's obvious that wherever they are that's their place, and wherever they go that's their way. Some birds, for example, migrate back to the same place year after year. No matter whether we call it unconscious or instinctive, that's their way. We also have our way, which we call the supreme way, the buddha way. That is to say, when we do one thing, we are complete in that moment. The way is right there, wherever we are. When we realize that this is the place and we are the way, practice follows naturally, spontaneously, and that practice is the genjokoan, the realization of ultimate reality.

"Attaining this place and this way." This place is the place where you really make yourself liberated and content. This way is the way of enlightenment, the buddha way. When you attain the way of enlightenment, your life itself becomes the enlightened life. We shouldn't confuse this "way" with some technique, or with some road for traveling someplace else. This way itself, this life itself, is realization. If we speak of realizing something else besides this life, again it's like putting another head on top of our own. To do very ordinary things in a very ordinary way — that's the buddha way.

One of the great Chinese Zen masters said, "Inwardly seeing your self-nature and being unshakable, indestructible, that's Zen." Mere physical sitting is not enough. You have to sit carefully and attentively. Let your body sit and let your mind sit. Let your emotions sit, let your breathing sit, let your blood circulation sit. Let everything sit. Then your sitting becomes indestructible, immovable. And when you really penetrate into it, it becomes more than that: the entire world in ten directions becomes one bright jewel. Nothing to move and nothing to be moved; nothing to destroy and nothing to be destroyed. That's zazen. As Master Dogen mentions elsewhere, don't just understand it conceptually, but understand it with your whole body and mind. When you practice in that way, your zazen becomes nothing but the unshakable, indestructible, enlightened state itself. Extending that practice into everyday life, your whole life becomes the enlightened life.

"Since this place and this way are neither large nor small, neither self nor other, neither existing previously nor just arising now, they therefore exist thus."

Since the realization of one's life is intrinsically with one to begin with, it is not newly arising. On the other hand, if you neglect practice, you won't realize the innate value of life. Since it's not "existing previously," you have to do something about it. The word "thus," then, is like the sharp, emphatic whack of a stick urging us to realize this wonderful thusness of life.

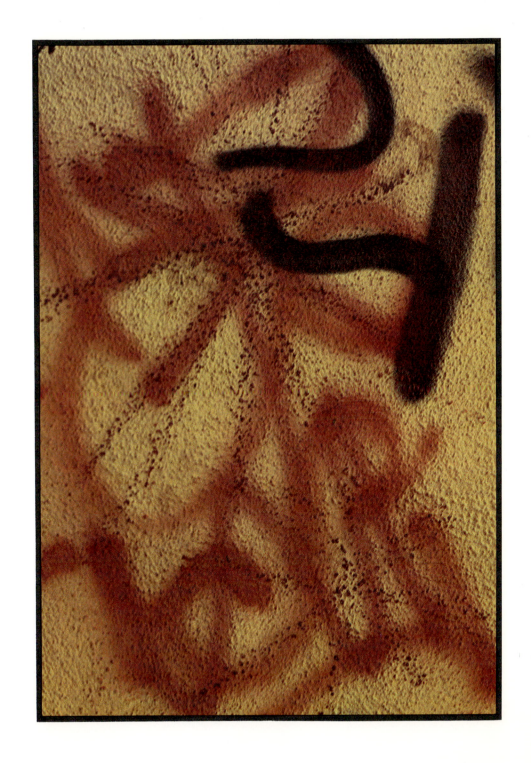

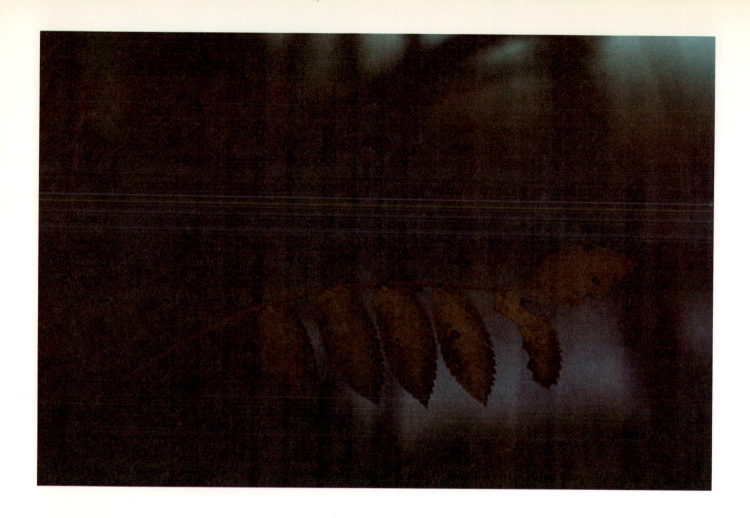

Since this place and this Way are neither large nor small, neither self nor other, neither existing previously nor just arising now, they therefore exist thus.

*Since the place is here and the way leads everywhere,
the reason the limits of the knowable are
unknowable is simply that our knowledge arises
with, and practices with, the absolute perfection of
the buddha-dharma.*

*Do not practice thinking that realization must become
the object of one's knowledge and vision and be
grasped conceptually.*

*Even though the attainment of realization is
immediately manifest, its intimate nature is not
necessarily realized. Some may realize it and some
may not.*

COMMENTARY ELEVEN

The meaning of this first sentence is similar to the meaning of the first sentence of the previous section. A fish that tries to find out how big the ocean is before swimming in it can't survive. We do that ourselves. We try to find out the limitations of our life before acting — it's simply impossible.

Similarly, some people think that until they complete their practice and attain enlightenment, they can't help other people. But such a time will never come, because practice is our life itself, and continues endlessly. So according to the demands of each situation, we do our best. That's our way.

"The reason the limits of the knowable are unknowable . . ." In the functioning of knowing in the usual sense, there is a dualism between the knower and the object to be known. But being itself is simply unknowable, for the same reason that the eye can't see the eye. It's all together one thing.

Then why does Master Dogen say, "Some may realize it and some may not"? Regardless of who realizes it and who does not, we are nothing but the dharma, the way itself. And yet definitely there is real enlightenment by which we attain the wisdom to see the boundary of the knowable, a wisdom quite apart from knowledge or conceptualization. In order to realize this wisdom we have to practice, which brings us to the monk's question and Priest Pao-che's reply.

*Do not practice thinking that realization must become the
object of one's knowledge and vision and be grasped
conceptually.*

Priest Pao-ch'e of Ma-ku shan was fanning himself. A monk approached and asked, "Sir, the nature of the wind is permanent, and there is no place it does not reach. Why, then, must you still fan yourself?" "Although you understand that the nature of wind is permanent," the master replied, "you do not understand the meaning of its reaching everywhere." "What is the meaning of its reaching everywhere?" asked the monk. The master just fanned himself. The monk bowed with deep respect.

COMMENTARY TWELVE

What's here right now!
Delusion is yesterday's dream
Enlightenment, tomorrow's delusion.

The monk is asking, Since we are nothing but buddha-nature itself, why is it necessary to practice? Dogen Zenji himself wrestled with this question for many years before finally resolving it once and for all. It was a commonly held view then and now that enlightenment is unnecessary because we are already enlightened. "The nature of wind is permanent and there is no place it does not reach. Why then must you still fan yourself?" But until we awaken to the fact that we are the life of the whole world, we won't understand its meaning. Actually, this awakening is the very essence of Buddhism.

"The nature of wind is permanent" means that all sentient beings are intrinsically the buddha. The monk's question is that since we are intrinsically the buddha, why do we need to practice?

"The master just fanned himself." Through activity, through practice we can vitalize and actualize our nature. True nature itself is rather static. We have to let it move, we have to let it revolve by our practice, by our activity. Then more and more the cheese of the long river will mature and ripen.

Please realize that your life is solid gold, and please polish it well. Make it shinier and shinier until shiny illumination itself disappears. This is the traceless enlightenment which continues forever.

"The master just fanned himself." Everything is right there. "The monk bowed with deep respect." Again, everything is right there. I am talking, you are listening — everything is right here. What more is there to seek outside of that?

"What is the meaning of [the wind] reaching everywhere?"
asked the monk. The master just fanned himself.

This is the enlightened experience of buddha-dharma and the vital way of its correct transmission. Those who say we should not use a fan because wind is permanent, and so we should know the existence of wind without using a fan, know neither permanency nor the nature of wind.

Because the nature of wind is eternally present, the wind of Buddhism actualizes the gold of the earth and ripens the cheese of the long river.

COMMENTARY THIRTEEN

Every day's a good day
Every hour's a good hour.

"Actualizes the gold of the earth and ripens the cheese of the long river."

This again refers to our life. "Actualizes the gold of the earth" means that we ourselves, our body, our mind, are nothing but the golden body of the buddha. Our life, however long or short, is enriched by proper practice and we grow all together into wonderful people.

"Cheese" is not an exact translation. The Japanese term *soraku* refers to a cultured milk drink popular in ancient China — perhaps "yogurt" would be closer. In any case, our whole life is a river which is slowly maturing and ripening, but unlike yogurt, over-ripening won't make us sour. The more sincerely we practice, the richer and smoother our taste will become.

In another essay, Master Dogen says, in effect, "If you wish to attain enlightenment, do zazen." When you do that, he says further, your treasurehouse will open of itself and you will use it at will. The gold of the earth will be actualized and the cheese of the long river ripened. That gold of the earth, that cheese of the long river of our life is our true nature. If we really practice, our wisdom will ripen and mature, and we will be able to function freely for the sake of all beings.

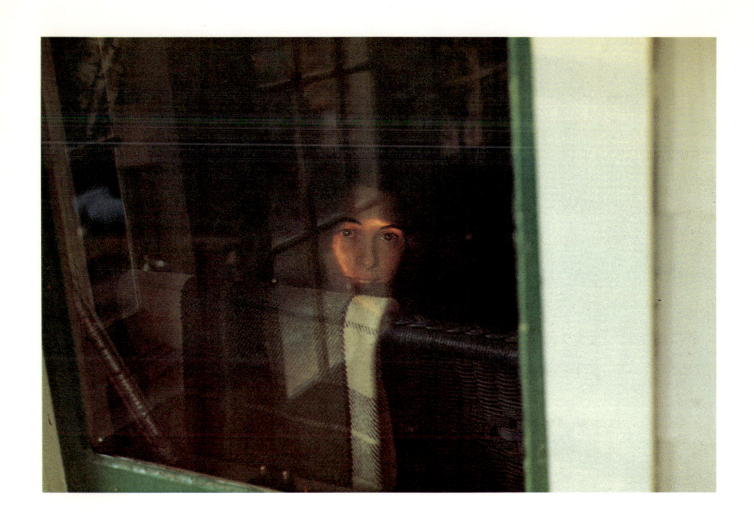

Because the nature
of wind is
eternally present,
the wind of Buddhism
actualizes the gold
of the earth
and ripens the cheese
of the long river.

A FEW TERMS DEFINED

buddha (Skt) (lit. "awakened one"): A term which variously indicates the historical Buddha Shakyamuni; enlightened persons; and the essential truth, the true nature of all beings.

dharmas (Skt): *Phenomena* is a close English equivalent, but seemed somehow excessively dry and abstract to capture the concrete quality of the original. According to Buddhist philosophy, dharmas — a term derived from the Sanskrit root "to uphold," thus giving it the sense of something enduring and indivisible — are the fundamental constituents of reality, psychological as well as material. The term *things* is sometimes used as an equivalent, but it is interesting to note that in Buddhism mental phenomena are no less real than things.

In the singular, dharma refers to the teachings of the Buddha, truth, universal law.

ten oxherding pictures: of ancient origin, they represent a step-by-step guide to the path to enlightenment in which the ox represents true nature. The pictures begin with the stage of searching for the ox, in which the desire to practice is awakened, and end with the return to the marketplace, in which the practicer transcends enlightenment and unenlightenment to function freely in the world of delusion.

zazen (J) (lit. "sitting meditation"): The practice of Zen meditation; in its broadest sense, the term zazen includes all activities carried out with mindfulness and wholehearted effort.

ABOUT THE PHOTOGRAPHS

As if I could give anything:
Take not images   *be*
Give not   *be*
Make not   *be*
Know not   *be image*
Count inhalations
       Count exhalations
Count nothing
       Be breath

      — Minor White

The photographs used to illustrate the commentary emerged from my work, study and practice under the guidance of Taizan Maezumi Roshi over the past sixteen months. Master Dogen's **Genjokoan** was my major preoccupation during this period of time. Through the formality of private interviews, casual conversations, study, and the foundation of Zen practice, sitting meditation — line by line, bite by bite, **Genjokoan** was examined, chewed, assimilated and tested in the clarity of Roshi's understanding. As each piece was approved I attempted to express that understanding or experience in a kind of visual capping phrase (a phrase used in Zen to epitomize a student's understanding) that would summarize visually, the way a capping phrase does poetically, the essence of that experience.

It has always been my feeling that somewhere between the words that describe it and the direct experience itself a space exists that is filled by the visual image, and when that image is perceived, in Master Dogen's words, "with the whole body and mind," then "one understands [it] intimately." If I have succeeded in keeping my "self" out of the way long enough for the camera to photograph, then these images are indeed Roshi's images and, in a special way, a twentieth-century manifestation of Master Dogen's vision.

                          John Daido Loori

LIST OF ILLUSTRATIONS

ABOUT THE CONTRIBUTORS

One of the most accessible and effective Zen masters in America today, **Taizan Maezumi Roshi** devotes his time and energy to his various functions as director and spiritual mentor of the Zen Center of Los Angeles and editor of the Zen Writings series.

Born in his father's temple in 1931, Maezumi Roshi was ordained a Soto Zen monk at the age of eleven, and after receiving degrees in Oriental literature and philosophy from Komazawa University, he studied at Sojiji, one of the two main Soto monasteries in Japan. In 1956 he came to the United States, studying English at Pasadena City College and at San Francisco State. Ten years later he founded the Zen Center of Los Angeles and began receiving students.

Maezumi Roshi has studied and received aproval as a teacher in both the Soto and Rinzai Zen traditions.

John Daido Loori is first and foremost a teacher of seeing. Director of Center Publications, he has been presenting lectures and workshops on Zen photography for the past eight years. His work has been extensively exhibited on the east coast, and has appeared in such publications as *Aperture* and *Time-Life Photography*. He studied photography with Minor White and Zen with Muishitsu Eido Roshi in New York, and is presently working on a book, *The Art of Mindful Photography*, to be published by Center Publications in 1979. He is currently studying Zen with Maezumi Roshi at the Zen Center of Los Angeles.

Vo-Dinh is perhaps the Vietnamese artist most honored outside his native country, from which he has been separated for many years. Born into a Buddhist family in 1933, he studied at the leading academies and schools of art in Paris, where he was also very active in the cause of peace for Vietnam. He now lives with his wife and two daughters in Burkittsville, Maryland.

 The paulownia leaves-and-flowers design is the trademark of Center Publications, publishers of fine books on Zen, Buddhism, the arts, comparative religion and related fields. Director: John Daido Loori. Editor: Stephan Ikko Bodian. Design: John Daido Loori. Graphics and Production: Larry Watson. Typeset in Tiffany by Dee Typographers, Los Angeles, CA. Printed and bound by Kingsport Press, Kingsport, Tennessee.